My Buddhist Year

Cath Senker

PowerKiDS
press.

New York

Published in 2008 by The Rosen Publishing Group, Inc.
29 East 21st Street, New York, NY 10010

First Edition

Picture Acknowledgments:
Art Directors & Trip Photo Library 11 (J. Moscrop), 27 (H. Rogers); Britstock 16 (Shiro Daifu), 17 (Sakae Arai); Chapel Studios 22 (Zul Mukhida); Circa Photo Library 6 (Tjalling Halbertsma), 8, 15, 19 (William Holtby); Clear Vision 12, 13, 18 (Mokshajyoti); Eye Ubiquitous *Cover* (David Cumming), 4 (Paul Seheult), 7 (Tim Page), 14 (Paul Seheult), 20 (Tim Page), 25 (Julia Waterlow), 26 (Tim Page); London Buddhist Vihara 21; Nutshell Media 5 (Yiorgos Nikiteas); Robert Harding Picture Library *Title page*, 9, 24; Tibet Images 10 (Ian Cumming), 23 (Robin Bath).

Cover photograph: A young Buddhist monk in Myanmar (Burma).
Title page: Young monks in Myanmar carrying the food offerings they have been given.

Library of Congress Cataloging-in-Publication Data

Senker, Cath.
  My Buddhist year / Cath Senker.
      p. cm. -- (A year of religious festivals)
  Includes bibliographical references and index.
ISBN-13: 978-1-4042-3730-8 (library binding)
  ISBN-10: 1-4042-3730-5 (library binding)
  1. Fasts and feasts--Buddhism--Juvenile literature. I. Title.
  BQ5700.S46 2007
  294.3'436--dc22
                          2006027571

Acknowledgments: The author would like to thank Carolina Rivas McQuire, Kelsang Shraddha, The Clear Vision Trust, the London Buddhist Vihara, Kishani Jayasinghe, the Venerable Kelsang Rabten and Jim Belither for all their help in the preparation of this book.

Note: The diary writer in this book, Carolina, is from the New Kadampa Tradition of Buddhism (NKT), an international Mahayana form of Buddhism that adapts to the culture of the country in which it is practiced.

Manufactured in China.

Contents

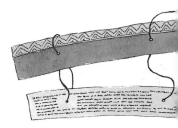

A Buddhist life

Buddhists follow the Buddha's teachings.
The Buddha was a great holy man.
He lived 2,500 years ago.

Buddhists follow some simple rules in their lives. They try not to kill or hurt living things. They try not to take anything they haven't been given. They aim to tell the truth and keep a clear mind. They try not to be greedy.

This is a statue of the Buddha at a temple in Thailand. The Buddha is always shown as calm and peaceful.

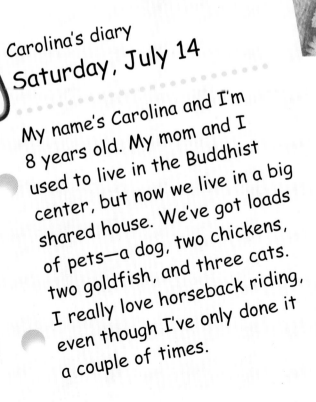

This is Carolina outside her Buddhist center. She has written a diary about the Buddhist festivals.

Carolina's diary
Saturday, July 14

My name's Carolina and I'm 8 years old. My mom and I used to live in the Buddhist center, but now we live in a big shared house. We've got loads of pets—a dog, two chickens, two goldfish, and three cats. I really love horseback riding, even though I've only done it a couple of times.

The Pali Canon is the oldest collection of Buddhist holy books. It contains the Buddha's teachings.

The Buddhist symbol is called the Wheel of Dharma.

Buddhist festivals

Buddhist festivals are joyful times.
People enjoy meeting together
at a Buddhist center or temple.
Everyone thinks about their beliefs
and how to become a kinder person.

There are many different Buddhist
festivals around the world. The most
important ones celebrate events in
the Buddha's life.

These Buddhist monks in Mongolia are celebrating the opening of a new monastery.

These girls in Sri Lanka are dressed in white for Poson Day.

Some festivals are special to a particular country. For example, Sri Lankans celebrate Poson Day. All Buddhists celebrate Wesak, or Buddha Day.

Carolina's diary
Sunday, August 15

We've just got back from our summer festival. It's my favorite Buddhist festival. It's for two weeks every year and we go camping. At the campsite, there are two big trees that I love climbing! I always meet lots of other children there who are Buddhists, too.

Special days

Every month

Every month, most Buddhists have special religious days. These are often days when there is a full moon. Many Buddhists go to the temple to worship.

Buddhist worship is called puja. People chant to show their love for the Buddha. They make offerings of flowers, candles, incense, and pure water at a shrine. People thank the Buddha for his teachings.

This man is worshipping in the shrine room of his Buddhist center.

In Colombo, Sri Lanka, there is a special ceremony on every full moon day.

Carolina's diary
Sunday, December 29

Yesterday was Lama Chopa (you say "Larma Cherpa"). This is a special day that happens every two weeks. I went to the children's group at the Buddhist center. We heard a story about the Buddha and talked about what it meant. We sang prayers. Afterward, we offered vegetarian food to the Buddha. We imagined him eating it. Then we had a feast and ate it ourselves!

A Buddhist teacher gives a talk and people meditate. They sit quietly and try to become still, relaxed, and peaceful.

New Year

January, February, March, or April

New Year is a good time for making a new start. Buddhists think about how to be more kind and generous to others. They may go to the temple to worship.

In Tibet, Buddhists spring clean their homes for a fresh new start to the year. Then there are three days of feasting, dancing, and sports. After this there are more serious ceremonies.

In Tibet, prayers written on colored flags are hung up as part of the New Year celebrations.

Carolina's diary
Friday, January 3

We held a puja on Wednesday to celebrate the New Year. I think of New Year like this: we believe in the power of karma, or actions. If you do kind things, you'll enjoy the results. You'll make the world a better place. For me, New Year is a time for looking at the last year and seeing how I could do better this year. Then I can make a fresh start.

In this village in China, women are taking part in a New Year dance.

In China, Sri Lanka, and Thailand, people also hold religious ceremonies. They enjoy special food, traditional games, processions, music, and dancing.

Parinirvana

February

At this festival, people remember the death of the Buddha. When he was 81 years old, the Buddha knew that the time had come for him to die. He lay down and died peacefully.

A painting of the death of the Buddha. The Buddha died with his friends gathered around him.

On this shrine, for Parinirvana, there are photos of loved ones who have died.

In the temple, the lights may be lowered. People chant and meditate in the dimmed light. Then the lights are made bright again. The lights are a symbol. They show that the light of the Buddha's teachings continues to shine in the world.

Carolina's diary

Sunday, February 15

My friend Ella invited me to visit her Western Buddhist center for Parinirvana. We heard a story about the last days of the Buddha's life. Then we talked about people we knew who had died. We put photos of them on the shrine. We always say special prayers for people who are dying so their next life will be good.

Magha Puja

February

At Magha Puja, Buddhists in Thailand and other countries remember an important event in the Buddha's life. This was when 1,250 of his followers came to see him.

He said they should try to be kind, generous, and patient. He said they should not harm living things.

In Thailand, people light candles and incense sticks at Magha Puja.

This young monk is meditating. Meditation is an important part of Buddhist life, and all festivals.

To celebrate Magha Puja, Buddhists go to their temple. In large temples, 1,250 candles are lit to remember the Buddha's followers.

Carolina's diary
Friday, February 28

Buddhists don't all celebrate the same festivals. Mom and I are NKT (The New Kadampa Tradition) Buddhists. We don't celebrate Magha Puja, but we do celebrate the teachings the Buddha gave to his followers. Every month there is the Kangso prayer. It celebrates our rules for everyday life. I don't go because it's four hours long and I'd get tired, but Mom does.

Hana Matsuri

April 8

Hana Matsuri is a Japanese festival. It celebrates the Buddha's birth. Buddhists wash a statue of the baby Buddha in perfumed water or sweet tea. They hang a garland of flowers around his neck.

The statue is paraded through the streets. Everyone throws lotus flowers into the path of the procession. Then there is a lively fair.

Children wear traditional Japanese clothes for the Hana Matsuri festival in Japan.

Carolina's diary
Tuesday, April 8

My friend Momo is Japanese. Today was Hana Matsuri and she e-mailed me about it. It's her favorite festival. She visited the temple, and there was a hall filled with colorful flowers. It looked like the beautiful garden where the Buddha was born. Inside was a lovely statue of the baby Buddha. Momo helped to pour sweet tea on the Buddha's head.

These children are joining in with the folk dancing at Hana Matsuri.

People set up stalls to sell food. There is folk dancing, and acrobats perform for the crowd.

Buddha Day

May

Buddha Day, or Wesak, is a very important Buddhist festival. It celebrates the Buddha's Enlightenment.

When the Buddha became Enlightened, his mind became clear and peaceful. He knew how to be kind to others, and how to help people to be happy.

This boy in Britain is lighting a candle at Wesak. The shrine is often specially decorated for the festival.

These Buddhists in Nepal are lighting lamps to celebrate Wesak.

At Wesak, Buddhists visit their temple to worship. Money or food may be given to poor people, and to Buddhist monks and nuns. Some Western Buddhists bring food and share a meal together.

Carolina's diary

Tuesday, April 15

Today was our Buddha Day. We went to the Buddhist center to be blessed. We were given a little woolen bracelet. Sometimes we get a crystal. We looked at it to remember the Buddha's Enlightenment, and to remember to love others. I'm going to wear my bracelet until it wears out. Then I'll put it on my shrine.

Poson Day

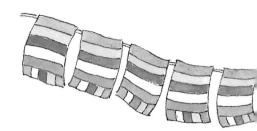

June

Poson celebrates the time when Buddhism came to Sri Lanka. Buddhists from Sri Lanka go to their temple. They listen to a talk. Then they chant and meditate together.

People make offerings and give money to the temple. It is a time to be especially generous.

These pilgrims have come to Mihintale, in Sri Lanka, to worship on Poson Day.

The Buddhist flag is raised outside a Buddhist temple in Britain for Poson Day.

Carolina's diary

Monday, June 24

Yesterday was Poson Day. My mom's friend Sarah told me how it was celebrated at a London temple. Lots of Sri Lankan people go there. At 9 a.m., they raised the Buddhist flag outside the temple. It was a very happy moment. After puja, chanting, and meditation they listened to a talk. Afterward they drank lots of tea and shared tasty Sri Lankan food.

In Sri Lanka, some people go on a pilgrimage to a place called Mihintale. This is where Buddhism first arrived in the country, over 2,000 years ago. An Indian prince told the king of Sri Lanka all about it.

Dharma Day

July

Dharma Day celebrates the first time the Buddha gave his teachings, called *Dharma,* which means "truth."

Buddhists believe that having things doesn't make people truly happy. They practice meditation. It helps them to understand that real happiness comes from learning to be happy with whatever we have, or whatever we are doing.

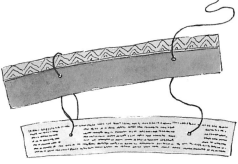

This monk is reading a story from the Pali Canon, which was written on strips of palm leaf.

These Tibetan boys are training to be monks. Reading the Buddha's teachings is an important part of their training.

On Dharma Day, Buddhists go to their temple. Children may listen to stories from the Pali Canon. They hear the Buddha's teachings about giving and sharing things.

Carolina's diary
Wednesday, July 6

Friday was our Dharma Day. We celebrated the Buddha's teachings spreading all over the world. We held a special puja. The Buddha taught people how to work things out for themselves rather than telling them what to do. Last week my friends were planning to run away from school. I talked to them about their reasons. In the end, they didn't leave.

Kathina

October or November

Kathina celebrates Buddhist monks and nuns. It began in Asia. Kathina comes at the end of the rainy season in Asia.

In Eastern countries, Buddhists look after the monks and nuns. They give them everything they need. This includes food, new robes, and shelter. Buddhists like to be generous.

These young monks in Burma are carrying the food offerings they have been given.

During the rainy season, monks and nuns stay in monasteries. When the rains stop, people give them new robes.

These monks are looking at the cloth they have been given to make new robes for Kathina.

Carolina's diary

Wednesday, October 27

It's good having a mom who's a Buddhist nun. When we're out, everyone can see that she's a nun, so she can't shout at me! Also, she's much calmer than she was before she became a nun. People don't give her new robes but they help in other ways. Last year, they gave her money so she could go to New York for some special buddhist classes.

Sangha Day

November

Sangha Day is a celebration of friendship. The Sangha is the Buddhist community. People like to gather with their Buddhist friends and teachers. They celebrate the love and support they give each other.

These children in Britain are meditating at their Buddhist center on Sangha Day.

Everyone enjoys having a meal together on Sangha Day.

On Sangha Day, people go to their temple. They may read from the Buddhist holy books and meditate.

Many people do puja and listen to a talk by a Buddhist teacher. Everyone enjoys a shared meal.

Carolina's diary
Sunday, November 9

Today was Sangha Day. We call it NKT Temples Day. We have temples in different countries where everyone can pray for world peace. On Sangha Day we do things to raise money for the temples. This year we had a show with people doing silly acts. You could pay money to throw cream pies at them! It was really funny. Then we shared loads of food.

Buddhist calendar

January/February/March/April

Buddist New Year

(1 day to 3 weeks in different countries) Buddhists think about how to be kinder and more generous to people.

February

Magha Puja (full moon day)

People remember how 1,250 followers came to the Buddha and were given a special talk.

February

Parinirvana (full moon day)

A festival held in memory of the death of the Buddha.

April 8

Hana Matsuri

A Japanese celebration of the Buddha's birthday.

May

Buddha Day or **Wesak** (full moon day)

An important festival to celebrate the Buddha's Enlightenment.

June

Poson Day (full moon day)

On this day, people remember Buddhism coming to Sri Lanka.

July

Dharma Day (full moon day)

A celebration of the first time the Buddha gave his teachings.

July/August

NKT summer festival (2 weeks)

NKT Buddhists gather to listen to teachings and learn about the Buddhist way of life.

October/November

Kathina (1 day)

A ceremony for giving new robes to monks and nuns.

November

Sangha Day (full moon day)

Buddhists come together to celebrate their worldwide community, the Sangha.

Glossary

Buddha The Buddha was called Siddhartha Gautama when he was born. After he attained Enlightenment he became known as the Buddha. The Buddha means "the one who understands the truth."

chant A prayer with a few words that are sung over and over again.

Dharma The truth. It also means the Buddha's teaching.

Enlightenment Being perfectly kind and generous, understanding the world completely, and being fearless.

incense A stick that is burned to give off a nice smell.

karma This means action.

meditate To sit quietly and still with your thoughts so you can become calm, happy, and wise.

monastery A special place where monks live together.

NKT The New Kadampa Tradition of Buddhism. It has many centers in Europe, the Americas, and Asia.

offerings Food, flowers, or other gifts that are placed in front of statues of the Buddha to give thanks for his teachings.

Pali Canon The oldest collection of Buddhist writings, from Sri Lanka.

pilgrims People who make a special journey to a holy place.

puja Worship.

robes Long, simple clothes, like the Buddha's clothes, that are worn by monks and nuns.

Sangha The group of people who follow the Buddha's teachings. Sometimes it is used to mean only monks and nuns.

shrine A place where people come to worship. It usually has an image of the Buddha. Many Buddhists have small shrines at home where they worship alone.

temple A building where Buddhists meet for worship. Some Buddhists call their temple a vihara. Others meet at a Buddhist center.

vegetarian food Food made without meat or fish.

Western Buddhist A Buddhist who is not from an Asian family. Western Buddhists may practice Buddhism in a different way from Asian Buddhists.

For Further Reading

Books to read

Buddhism (Religions of the World)
by Anita Ganeri
(World Almanac Library, 2006)

Buddhism (World Religions)
by Mel Thompson
(Walrus Books, 2005)

Buddhist Stories (Traditional Religious Tales) by Anita Ganeri
(Picture Window Books, 2006)

Buddhists, Hindus and Sikhs in America (Religion in American Life)
by Gurinder Singh Mann (Oxford University Press, USA, 2002)

The Kids Book of World Religions
by Jennifer Glossop
(Kids Can Press, 2003)

World Religions (History Detectives)
by Simon Adams
(Southwatwer, 2004)

Places to Visit

Asian Art Museum

200 Larkin Street

San Francisco, CA 94102

Tel: 415.581.3500

www.asianart.org/

The Tibetan Museum Society

114 South Patrick Street

Suite 1

Alexandria, VA 22314

Tel: 703-836-1773

www.tibetan-museum-society.org

Due to the changing nature of Internet links, Powerkids Press has developed an online list of Web sites related to the subject of this book. This site is updated regularly. Please use this link to access the list:
www.powerkidslinks.com/ayrf/buddhist

The author

Cath Senker is an experienced writer and editor of children's information books.

Index